PRAISE for Jennifer H. Fortin's

WE LACK IN EQUIPMENT
& CONTROL

Jennifer H. Fortin is the Walt Whitman of the month of February, the curator of apartment environments, the weatherman of goodbyes, a dewy-eyed automaton, the impresario controlling the hunger artist and the hunger artist herself, Bernadette Mayer's daughter watching out of an eye corner as her mother writes *Midwinter Day*, the miracle body rescued from three days in a snowdrift, still, alive, still alive. She gives us poems of scraps and details and lets us make something—big and vital—from her materials. When I read these poems I feel as if I am accumulating "not data but a song."

Darcie Dennigan

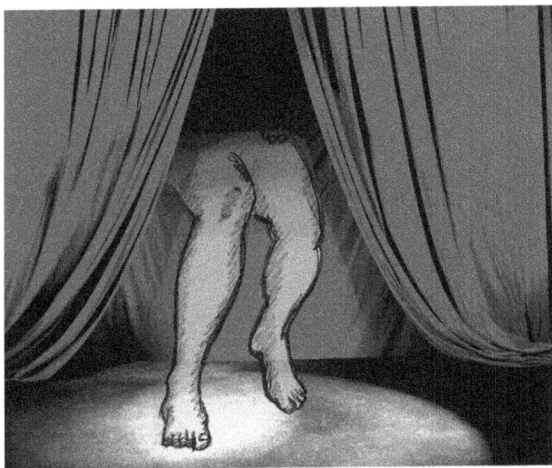

John Dermot Woods

Also by Jennifer H. Fortin

Mined Muzzle Velocity

WE LACK IN
EQUIPMENT
& CONTROL

WE LACK IN EQUIPMENT & CONTROL

Jennifer H. Fortin

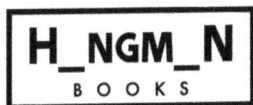

H_NGM_N
BOOKS

www.h-ngm-nbks.com

FIRST H_NGM_N EDITION, August 2013

ISBN 978-0-9882287-1-9

Book layout by Nate Pritts
Cover by Greta Hambke

For a complete listing of titles, visit
www.h-ngm-nbks.com

For more on this book, visit
www.h-ngm-n.com/lack

TABLE OF CONTENTS

i. of environmental concern

ii. that which just gets tired & then kind

FOR NATE PRITTS

WE LACK
EQUIP
&
CONT

IN
MENT

ROL

I.

OF
ENVIRONMENTAL
CONCERN

A great snowstorm & maybe
you will not apologize
for the details you use in order
to sponsor your other details.
Snow a giant detail I want
to point out, but there's now no one
living with me. How fast
each morning alarm, although I'm faster.

Taking liberties we aren't comfortable with
You said my scent had changed (long before February), whose
        immunity?
I would like sustainability, an agreement entered into
I would like you to go eat breakfast especially hearty
I can't be any plainer
Here was your love
Everybody can get you out of it
It is difficult to be a person
The atmosphere will save & share our searches, neurobehavioral
Use the same phrases each time, this will harden
The polluting elements,
They're the ones you curate again & again

There are ten suns
in today's forecast.
I'd like to see this happen, ten
discrete appeals. I'm not even
on vacation. Does the older
one recede & to whose
pocket, does the new one
fit perfectly on top, collateral.
The moon should arrive all
at once, allegiance to tablature
some fastidious person bothered
to diagram. What evening force
there's no saying. It could be
the score of a green fireball
tearing open the sky. Chaos
& crowding are certain.
It feels like no one save me
scrambles about the atmosphere.
Maybe this is the smartest way
to get ready for the end, as you are,
calmly, bathing, inclination of what
not to wear. We could be the first
state to criminalize lists titled
Goodbye. Any word is very
capable of being safe, you only
have to agree on it beforehand.
I'll pass on your lesson & refrain
from your sleeves. Yours then
mine then yours. Ownership
iteration the learning of
a foreign forever. Some mimicry is
necessary. That's a thing people
do, learn foreign forever.
They do necessary. Another
thing they do is evolve
independently into species.
& touch columns with Wet
Paint signs. Make port stops
in order to say I've been,
when they could just say.
Those you prove the excursion

to don't care so much
as to form reconnaissance
patrols. We hope when we
dispose of something
it enriches the environment.

Finishing off tasks, food, but not films, we began together
Sometimes I'm just on February hoard vacation
Then I remember
If you return, might it be because you have no-
where else to land, a small plane lowered
onto the turnpike between cars
I can't say I won't turn to look like everyone else

D. likes to home
video the home
being built
&, before,
the boat. It was
essential for me
to ask who *you*
was in his narrations,
but I couldn't.
I turn green
in February from
rocks, no matter
if gentle as
a shell & shelter, gutted.

I found out on the pointed projection,
the surface of this new year

(tho it's February, the brief-
est, my entrance upon state)

from our (our) friend:
boys have no idea until they do

that most women groom their eye-
brows. Thought women

simply are shapelier.
What news follows you these days?

What impresses you?

For me it's been textural, mostly burlap, fat
& felt. It is my snow, so it is my problem.

I've been surrounding   myself

with friends, I've never   talked   more

            about friends. I like   how   they stalk

            when I most need it,   February.

They eat   with me, b/c friends know   I can't

turn it down.   We turn our   collars

toget-   her, my friends   & I, so   the inner

            is the outer. One   of my   very important friends

swarmed   my red until my   head was the very mean

            of the woolen warm   rose,

            the part I believe   you   can't   touch   or

the petals at once   fall off, over-   friendly.

I was alright   then, at least   for a bit, &   immodest.

Since the waking & rerestraint, honor brings you to various basins with me. Dip into the pending, the runoff testing what we can't see. In these quarters we bookmark & trade tiles, value unappraised. We share a glass after just having met, & accordingly I let myself anticipate cresting (river, chest, tuft, process of prominence). Neither looks the moment china is dropped, but the girl raises her hand to accept blame, further, to announce it, her arm a savage calyx protecting more of what we can't see. One night's miniature redux fast-forwards so it's as though we greeted goodnight & good morning, the grotto of our sleep had us waking, sleeping, waking, & so on, so it was as though we had counted many nights together instead of one. I need to think more & more specifically about periodic states.

Let me hold your public hand, a breezeway. The best way to insert wires or needles, depending on profession, is through the inconspicuous separation. Most days I am arrested in the city I claim to have hand-tied. What's worse than the thing not working out is when it is freshly-turned. A reason from the corner, you deem it seedling. Arrows perpetually defer from & to the opening. There's this geometry above the knees, it basically dictates: trust the depression at the end opposite the stem.

owner called, i didn't answer because i was asleep, but she left no
message, i got anxious that somehow i was her last hope

one of our friends slept in the blue sleeping bag (it wasn't yet
        february)

lakes wine replenished

i'm not here nearly as much as you'd expect, i awaken thickly

you missed e.'s puppets, swoons over ivories

tickets are going, we won't get them b/c we can't talk quickly
        enough

i never go to the gym, in lieu i duck into the running joke

i rarely indicate, however we are definitely february, when
        was the first of february

i will meet the youngest person yet after work, wash hands, quiet
& try not to let on for the sake of his unattached skull

The signs urge you to Get Help In Over 50 Languages. Not necessarily what I would recommend. There will be sport. Roman numerals & streaming. Precise predictions regarding behavior under stress. There's something locustlike or even sexual continuously happening in the spirit of assault. I am allowed thru all gates if I bring along environment in February. I can go out & come back in again whenever you desire spectacle, just say *edict*. I don't want anyone to honor my day length, to assist with trademark issues. Today should likely include Champagne but instead, defeat campaign. The sound was pure accident, which is assurance that you'd be lucky to guess wrong.

The awl responsible for our strains of music has been tossed
The warning has been downgraded to advisory

The ticks in shoulder-high grasses have detected my carbon
dioxide, completely occupied with blood

The official can't decipher my recurring nightly mares
Code-name the secret ghost settlement with a number

& the name of a nearby city, & I'll still manage to hang mobiles
       & reorganize
The prerequisites have vanished, in their place recruiters
       forge menus

Beat into shape your food-handling practices
Consider the salt spread over the roads the previous night

February pedals onto the scene affiliates I don't want to meet
Free to run or overrunning?

Chat Live With Our Meteorologists,
the web counsels.
About the weather, I suppose,
but can I also mention my various
hang-ups. I mean, how many of these atmo-
spheric scientists have never had their heart-
venue switched after the programs
were printed/switched the venue after
the programs were printed of one or more
hearts. Or made literal note of the pale gift-
wrapped display boxes tacked up behind the post
office staff & just wanted
to drop out of all lines forever, bareback overhaul.
If you see opportunities for collaboration, yell.

Not my task to keep track, who's upright
I like track fire, overtaken apartment
complex, near-ranch conditions
There's a symmetry that thrums but is virtuoso
Which proves I'll be okay or great, even in February

The clouds correct us precipitous, then compliant
They do not evoke simile with lonely or whathaveyou
The Romantic day has passed, I never feared
water & won't start now
A worthy light coming into being again restores
People look twice or just once for a long time
Wishing they had such good ideas

I have to remind you
it makes me feel
like an electronic medium,
& not pleasantly, when
someone says he'll pray
for me. Tables ordered
chockablock in
a room, each with a telephone,
person on one end, presumably
person on the other.
What an askew lair.
Surprise distracts
in the extreme, as when pain
succumbed to the man tap dancing
in the inappropriate setting.
I'm crossing it all, taking
objects made in private
so only the maker knows
their composition & purpose.
You own a personal perverse
plastic so snug you extract it
during red rituals. You should
carry it, abject, when you travel
& occasionally brandish
to indicate association.

Bless you, first speech of the day
Then trafficking in fuses, the market teems
for fuses as artery & vein replacement
Let dumb injuries be a matter of public record
When I ask the intern if he's doing alright, he always says yes
& returns the question more carbonated, I ask often
I devise the means to transmit large abstractions without
        compromise
I turn formats into formats, my boss thinks it genius, we're
        all geniuses
I work on intrusion detection systems while jotting unlit
        messages
Like this we avoid audits & cannons

Assigned a task force: the distinct vortex is twice
the size of our largest state at this point. After you
have read the letters, hoard them between magazines,
be strong as a roll of paper charged
by possible fire, & stronger. Here comes extinction,
without warning. We went from pistols to necklaces
to necklessness without pause: no wonder I chatter
about corruption, o neck-on-the-line. When electric
light was novel, depiction of nightlife was too.
Technology augmented, augmented our documentary
with its greens & anything-but-greens. When elec-
tric light was a novel, we discovered the embedded
by negative space. I only wish there
were any inkling of your side, its meaty seams.
Let's exchange professional reticence,
I am more than ready. Signal to me from
the battlefield, even if it be sea, with the white fan,
touch shore several times in heightened semaphore.

I check in   even   other people's homes   the burning
The cleaning lady in yesterday's   home walked   in on me,
no   pretending I   wasn't
doing what   I was doing
I rest   when I can
Adjust the level   for what   isn't there
                                   Winds   from
a direction, stimulation   of pixels
It's good to compute gross   tonnage; or it's the
only   thing that's worked for me   Quantify,
resuscitate, we   do indeed reside   in space
          My orbits are skirt-   ing the fact of
February,
                    this anniversary that isn't   Adjust the
          level, hike it
I rest when I   can
Unlikely inspiration has me   killing it,
                         going for it,

doing it,
breaking legs
There are grammars we assure   each other,
                         sore throttle, full throttle or no
Rest when you can

We weren't sure whether the garment the actor wore while shot in her worst film should go into the auction. That was the last we saw of her. An act of faith is the painting pressed between. An act of faith is correspondence longer than letters. Venting the lethal, it's not either/or. We count the interval between this worst & the last. Part of my time on the clock consists of opinion. Some elegance was in making it to kneel at the toilet, the union my hair forms. Call me by the name of a company when you feel abandoned in leagues. Contamination is a way of life, the personal struggle preceding critical success.

These guys captain admirable ships, but I don't
anticipate service to match. They are being shipped,

the first has already come. The machine who kicks

off the day. The machine who worms a day off.
The one who will answer my calls when I am
drunk or beat. Who will divide the critics,
reduce my assignment,

weed out the rookies with his own tender-
footed, but not overly tenderfooted, air.

That one knows we still have to intrigue
to a degree our scrubbed February tundra.

Let's start with a pocket-sized radar. A radar
whose development several inventors contributed to.

We publish our crying on cruise lines, on trains, walking,
driving because there are places to be &/or we can't get off.

Shoulder-season departures occur just before or after
the holidays. These departures are related to the rugburn
on my shoulder. We can imagine how that got there.

On land you are able to hear the speaker turned on
even in the absence of amplification. Noiseless noise,
an object's body language. Research suggests you
should not expect the same onboard.

In the unpleasant event that you snore, which upsets February's
breadth: you will be encouraged to don a device around
your jaw to support with silence your slumber's athleticism.
We aren't interested in obstacles.

Crying in your pulled-over car, on the road to nowhere
extraordinary, when the cop shines his light in, asks
if you're okay, you never know how to answer.

Although its accounts take great   care,
            there's a journal I know of that, when
full, is   waste. Another party   digging sent
                  one back to our keeper, who trashed it again.
Disposal crown, someone found the expulsion
bad enough to assert   flare. Off to meditate
                  fleet management. Were it   my journal
I would list   obligations the fleet owner   should
stick to. To use   the wreath. To cough up the   aerial
            photos. To revise: controversial permission
                  into permission. Disclose the purpose of
the bags of corks. Remove   the hold placed on me.

Snow melts lately placing in our care
again its borrowed garbage, plastic-skinned
What did snow learn of pedigree from our elimination
If we had landlines I could vow objectivity
I am tired of being polite
I might send you something unasked-for
I have a poor idea of portion
Do you know what the equator is?
I should express remorse but there's a nucleus
You were promoted to many fish, predator & prey
Unfavorable mutations selected against

Do you know what the equator is? Yes, it separates the earth

Call me placed like accident. Vial brine done done. Verify accident & nature name. Remains balm, agree the dusty rose dress, high-collared. Prop her, the hair done. Bone smarts the dusty risen into rebreathing. Don't worry about not being able to move or fall off. We'll have a long talk after this. It was colder rather than motorcade. Maybe wed, a side to whose. Get a cramp & drive suggestion. The cod intimated to table. She a pillar to the service. He, no one is as comfortable as no one looks. The looking the most influenced & therefore comfortable, agoraphobic flight from manipulation. I nostalgic eat, underwater mesh a regular cut from behind. Concerto in rethought, tendentious upon tendentious. When finally safe & effective, only a few behind thee & gaining. For I would approach blame toward the liable image. Tautological murder comes to mind.

Spring has one thing to offer, a breach that husks us
The world's first rhyme will someday come back around,
governed by the unimpeachable, by such mad & marvelous
graces as the whitest wave, & even more so,
should this assumption prove consistent, what serendipity,
if not, looting & banditry, hidden expenses, sabotage
of savings, you ought to roll up the tarmac, get a territory
February accelerates in dog years, its distances lightyears
You ought to hold me at arms' length for the administration
You ought to ask if I was one of the storm's thousands powerless
When we met, your reflex was to flood the village,
create a dam for power, we were made jealous

of the bell tower, the only sound above water
You ought to be told that drought uncovered the village,
even while snow invested in its squall, unheard of environment
Cancelled ground doesn't budge now, healthy
From here on out I customize the uncovered mouth
This is where men work around me at my request
Where men trade evacuation maps for provocation itineraries
This is where men expose the top ten fields losing people fast
Since their perimeters touch, except the outermost,
it's really one field losing people

II.
THAT
WHICH
JUST GETS
TIRED
&
THEN
KIND

Of the alleged event of our having broken
the back of the colony
Indisputably it's the gait cajoles us to stop

Think the world has ended, not sure.

Suggestion: we reposition ourselves in more genial industries.

Turns out getting rid of things in a moral fashion is

               harder than we thought.

I had the room darkened in order to tell your temperature
      by hue, by the cover, you're not hiding.

I hope to see you on the beach at the next ship breaking.
      Not like breaking a green horse,

which just gets tired & then   kind.

The cartouche you gave me doesn't anymore represent

      my name. It wore into a small arm

's powder which I will corrupt when most called for.

Do you love your horse but are scared. I have found   you

can attempt to measure in days of training, but you can never
      know

how many
        before
                 you tried the basics (using hands to stroke

back, neck, head). In passing behind a horse,

      angel or boat

on the cusp of ruin, touch your body

to its. When bodies compare thusly, there's no length a strike

has to go before landing. Seems more dangerous to be right
      up against,

but it's actually
                 safer, dizzyingly so.

It could be snow in the streetlamp
glow or summer insect
madness. I can't judge period
of year because I've reached
this conclusion: we're aglow
from our recesses, not outside.
Whiteout redevelops, not
unforeseen, even the plows are off the roads.
This snow makes the books.
Toilet paper & flashlights make the books.
The grown man is without exception
more comfortable with interactions on the left
side of his body—it's not data but a song.

We had recently watched a special, remember, the dead
whale on a truck bed exploded everywhere. They held out
until the end to express the cause.
I was asleep before the end,
exhausted from not having laid hands on
anything since that breed on the active island.
Why do they stampede back restless? & from.
Stampede coming & coming, in & out.
You reported the end of the special like you were posing
for a bust. Who is a relay race participant.
February is a black cold baton passed among teammates.

The dreams of animals & women waive the obscene. & men? My last bleeds into industry. The temperature I pretend to be in charge of & I, we hope to be an exception to the policy we guess into you. Friction need not be repealed. As long as you want my most green horse, my most real, take my horse blanket. I'll lead her to your room & leave her, you asleep as calorie. We throw around calories like they are physical entities, not units. Emergency organizations are not accepting donations. People with everything taken: basic needs can be forgiven. There's a type of knot you need to know if you can be found crouching near fetlocks, stunned by unmitigated flexion. If you respond to sweated shying away. Persuade my meals into three dimensions. If, whatever you're astride, I am drenched. The knot is willing to negate itself—a visual effect—to resolve a brittle spooked.

Horses versus canonized: not unprecedented. The historic weather stranded. The Associated Press states that even if you're careful, pharmaceuticals can end up in the water. Snow is infinitely more hormonal than we suspected. It throws me off, bloodstream cravings & moods. Upheaval, empathetic with the feminized fish. Black bath. Every day I take three tabs minimum. Let me tell you about absorption. I was able to learn properties after a night of disquiet. This fact does not depend on a point of view. Am I supposed to create a Facebook now. Engaging in text messaging is asking for trouble, particularly as the day breaks. There isn't snow. Our obstruction, our entertainment, our momentary logo. I'm busy taking a hard look.

Plexiglas has supplanted the ruining fence around the flame. It was a question of focus. There was no choice in the hosting, but there was a choice to love. See how it gets restored, discordant stewards, white-gloved, escorting us to our cabins. "Poor judgment," not misconduct, claims the aide. Where before I'd call back each nut & bolt from our time apart, gather & give them to you in an unsealed envelope, now there are impressions I hurl onto the summit, out of view until the future brakes or probably until always. As a child I hated eggplant for how it was put together (not for the thing itself), picked them from the garden & hurled those bad boys on top of the shed. As though they'd borne the brunt in their bed & now would live a refined existence off the grid. If that's not decadence then what is. It's a question of focus. The origin of "brunt" is perhaps the Middle English *sexual assault*, akin to heat, akin to itch.

Scholarship the bale I trace & tie with cords, defensive
gut attitude. For once I'd like to be given a good Feeling
Faces Chart with suitable emotions accurately labeled.
Drawbacks include overexcitement/confusion.
There are drawbacks to February living.
I've never performed so many lively functions
& honestly don't want to start now.
The sanitation department is snarled up
in my snow drifts, therefore is also snarled up
in my quickening trophy.

Pull a tax maneuver to gain commodity, ask your representative
       about new deductions
Recurred frost phenomenon
Not every horse's head winds a towel, you twistneck, obtuse
       angle the yield
of fragile rein compression
Extract the sap using similar slight compression, we'll turn
       90 degrees minimum
& test for matching type

Anger over aid mounts

There is a February foal turning into me, feed
my nails to the barn dogs or any dog who wants 'em
That's nail clippings, feed my nail clippings
Don't measure me to withers—my head, periscopic
       hindrance, does count
We'll take president holiday no matter our politics, no matter
       our Olympics
My class in the faraway place was confused by this business
of whether or not the animal sees its shadow,
& kind of enchanted

o human relevance, you vessel

Meanwhile, vigorous
growth in my hotbed
Stakes for bedposts,
a couple of parallel burnt nights
Weave past the judge,
we're almost enough
to require a parade

Supposedly I'm building a new body
& preparation is not wise,
it's just taking care
Will the teeth come in as slowly
Will it have two hearts, better
filtration, does it have more
or less sexual intercourse with you
I'd surmise the permit is in
the wash of this new
body, its lashes out
Did the ponies from my other
sections obtain permission
Do they build new bodies later

You'll sleep less as you age. The relative repeats that my little back was so straight. A girl I didn't know well & I took a paint & a palomino down by the pond bank & swapped. It was my idea. Hers didn't follow directions well. Strirruped, wanting it so bad, some invisible blacksmith in no time shod the moment in potential. Sleep wasn't easy that night either, but must have arrived eventually.

Your shoes by the door.
The milk gone bad, dated a smeared February.

Ate dinner once   again last   night, ancillary

Large green   bolts

Very female, wondered about   the natural

impulse for halos   of feather

The female can   be   responsive to   appropriation

of its   traditions, locate your   own sweat

lodge

Technically,   etiquette seals the energy-

efficient   bays

There's a storm   tracker   avail-   able online,

get the facts diminished

Have   I   convinced you

of the rare supple-

mental   What items champion in February & whose pointed

doubts

Impossible to report   to your post

of duty if you don't distinguish

the chief   expectations, wild   finicky   dose

currency &/or services to exchange for the goods in mind
surface devotion
motivated love or bluer mutilation thereof
that familiar bright-dry deficit
a knife—sufficient for inevitable sudden calculus—honed by
        restitution
implements from the deep completely sure of their inner lives
        (see: let bowl play swollen stadium)
abused modern fire you therapeutically flatter
        to the point of unfaltering loyal flush
neural wherewithal
your particular spice pace
protein quotient, disqualified plant
luscious texture-aggregate (simply called
        "Protect" in northern regions)
partial ego withdrawal

I would never say

what actually is.

                Nervy as congress.   Press the nerve

& reaction. Hostage

       of assembly or freedom

             of nerve. It's your

turn, your lot   turned by intent   to weapon.

I urge you,   nervous all-

                y, to fight

for my agenda.

According to the searcher of my person,
I have settled the fact of hooves fully
off the ground at a gallop, pull, push, tuck
Painting, a choice, inevitably
priming red, working big
In savage solidarity
call my elsewhere friends, tell them
I've been delicate & don't want to be
The configuration has changed
due to our chemicals, easily I like you
right now, flat deal w/ a solitary gentle
brief allusion, w/ audiovisual share
The reward will be organic, since January
I'm not a tough sell
The reward could incorporate pubic hair,
which is not tacky despite my public high
school art teacher's instruction otherwise
All our nudes shaved, the price of spring
goods in the dead of winter
We are not automatic
Volley back the grenade at your feet,
but was the command interpreter mere vault
Is it bravery if means for survival
If you'd like to meet my mind should I
bring an envoy body, as we learned in sex
ed & maybe in life, the brain is
arguably our most important sex
organ, & according to the searcher of my person,
I look like a repository for everything done blue b/c I am

As others see us, the vertigo
worsens. You used to have lodgings
in the stable. Our symptomatic
analogy displaces the turn
to our surroundings. Is the arsenal
weaponed with newborns, difficult
fruit shooting from lozenges,
things made. Would you describe
it as dockyard, the wharves
your fingers carving
disease from my seas.
Those of us who did not beg are condemned
to blaming & blaming the orbit.
There is something none of them is
keeping from us, try as they might
to abide by their shared veil.
What little remains lamentably deploys.
Fine motors privilege a fuel
we're not used to.
I had a tremendous encounter
with my angel. Our devastation
was complete & noble as naval
service. She handed off my
notice, I answered freely.
My birth was the end of an age,
any nurse would raise her voice
in assent. I trust one undivided word,
it emanates from my angel's
wintery plexus. The word is also
the author of the list. Each
utterance not true
at the tribunal. *I wonder whether
to like,* I thought, before
the solace-rise, brutally
curious regarding
liking's learning. When
I speak of you it is as bucking
from my general, robust fondness.

I walk a sickle around the man in my path
He is casting paper napkins to the ground with dark conviction
This is not what I need
when I'm trying to get back to where I live
I don't need to recognize dark conviction
The faint & high-pitched scene sends me over some edge
Doesn't he understand sickle is not tourniquet,
there's this ability of the sharp catch when you are
swaying along, medics do not maintain our grasses
I've aligned myself & that's not salve coating
my implemented rut, it's a softer substance, threatening

Thyroid of inferior
glass, I can't
metabolize the mental
nor the physical.
The races are on,
the hounds apparently
off, the hair
doing what. My
best friend will
tell you, &
I love her
as you care
in times of
emergency. One omits,
we can assume
others will compensate.
The men do
indeed depict their
mistresses but dance
around doing it
naked. The women
refine others' essences,
you would agree.
My dear, I
demand everything here
in the convention,
as you might expect.
This is your
signal. Gather in
our tight tract &
swallow. Make your
awesome camp in
the center of
my dry district.

Who's the more skilled decorator
It's he who should helm from day to day in February
It's he who should be held accountable when the deck is found
not to be water-tight
Figure in extrinsic agents as well as the artifacts they produce:
statistic, object, result or other
He who should calculate optimal passenger capacity
He who should make arrangements for our freight
For the embarrassment of embargo
From satellite facility earn me by interval
Square outstanding fines, really understand omega

I've issued a compulsory recall of green
horses, the entire production run.
Established a hotline, taken out ads.
The untrained should not participate
in reform. Everyone keeps telling
me how great the next thing will be. Luck. Patience.

I reckon I'll be hit harder.

Illusion of the separate. I'll hire a man to keep
slapping them up, new corridors by the minute.
I hereby have accommodated warranty, & you, & relevant
liability: I give up. Experts admit the recall may not
totally fix safety problems. I want what's mine,
what I've earned with my trouble.

I'm not proud of myself, calling my own hotline,
shutting out the following poor bastard conceived
on an improvised bed of saddles. He's only trying to
abide by the law, help with the recovery.

The country's grief continues
in a stream of letters addressed
to structural you, cataract
of letters. Cull those occluding
& replace with artificial.
The opposite of a person's
hate is impossible to hull,
although tempting. Shipwreck
discoveries are not as stirring
as they used to be, but
the proportion of ocean
life is more stirring than ever.
My friend the buccaneer wanted me
to see an article not for the article
but for the cover of destruction.

Only fierce like
this anymore.
Switch back
& forth between wind-
ows, portray arch-
itecture to familiarize
yourself with
new locale. It has
always worked for
me in the past. & you
see my patterns
are visible only when
polished. It takes an elbow
or two, the eternally
obvious. Allow, allow.
We will meet
at the market
dressed as men
to attract
less
attention from
the dealers & buyers.

The tightening effect, the brace. Visible storage attracted
        audience.
Humidity at restrained levels. Grouped by material,
the intelligence of somebody's belongings bridled.
The most relished ones fixed to sliding doors
you can pull out if you're aware. Your palette
these days makes you appear. Which is
the background & which the foreground.
My unfinished work reveals method.
There are locks in your hair.
Hearing or reading the street's name
will sadden me after you go, & there's an outdated ship
        who stomps in wait.
A friend from the foreign place carpeted the stairs of my child-
hood home without permission. He wore a mask
to prevent the broadcast of his exhalations.
The mask also blocked out certain
portions of the floor before he began work.
Will you just block out with me.
Sometimes I look up & see people coordinating as though
        there's solidity.
They don't mind me, the blank retriever. Gloss over everything
in storage, give it a nurse's uniform. She really didn't
develop into much. Our green horse has
triumphantly returned. He'll do that
from time to time, unconsciously
sensing where his body & limbs are,
sensitive to flies. We have trained specialists
to interact with certain creatures. We lack in equipment
        & control.

Legwork is underway. So begins our pitch & court of the light's deepening. My pulse did not budget for this concussive rush. We can't or won't go back. In borrowing, there are plans for a next time implicit. Our respective horses sense the two ditched but deeply-nested storms & might take a shot at collapse. Collapse deep brackish, recirculate. Divert the private eye who superimposes a transparent sheet on top of markings, does the same to the breed & then sex. Some of us do what we say we will do. Monitor your indirect footfall pattern. I believe there is a leg to stand on. Could the private eye be witness. Hot-bloodedness feels to me like the edge of your childhood gorge, where I've never been & refuse to imagine.

Boat run aground, gaps emerge in census
Watch for signs of overheating & further propeller spoilage
There's evidence of rocks, covered evidence
Let's assume you are more fortunate
Our bulbs are acute & shielded
A fresh coat of arms, wear me into a year ago
People have stories they tell, they want
me to run the threads
My boss has a friend who's on the wall
in the kitchen
Disturbed image
until renegade her friend climbed down my brain
& became photograph on the wall
Still disturbed image
My former fellow expat's solution
is to flee, wants to look for
the most terrible thing we can find
together
You wanted placid of late
I went up, the pressure felt nice
Skipped lines, it's not the season
Gold religion roofs stood up, & projects
On the way back from horses before you
we gave a girl a lift home
We can't all ride one horse
To the inanimate we go to really get places
People think
these are projects, but they're not
How she spoke was vitamin
But it sounded nice, like correct elevator pressure,
to be working on something long-term
together
Maybe like the most terrible thing we can find
The others up there stopped
whenever they wanted, it made me furious
I was trying to memorize the best routines
They were selling at every corner of the ascent, it was
easy to say no
Thank you thank you thanks no
Rejection awfully close to gratitude
In the photos people want specific engineering
as background, I want no background, but green, inexperience,
black or February
There's a humiliating construction behind you, turn around

WE LACK
EQUIP
&
CONT

IN MENT

ROL

ACKNOWLEDGMENTS:

Thank you to Carl Annarummo, who published some of these poems as a Greying Ghost pamphlet.

Thank you to Drew Swenhaugen and Marshall Walker Lee, who, at Poor Claudia, published most of the section *That Which Just Gets Tired & Then Kind* as a chapbook.

Thank you to Greta Hambke, John Dermot Woods, and Darcie Dennigan for the brightness you add here.

Thank you to the editors of the following journals, who published some of these poems in some iteration: *The Cossack Review, Country Music, Esque, H_NGM_N, LIT, Mud Luscious, Paper Darts, Redivider*, and *So and So Magazine.*

And thank yous heaped on top of thank yous to my family and friends. You know who you are and for what.

We Lack in Equipment & Control is Jennifer H. Fortin's second book. Lowbrow Press published her first, *Mined Muzzle Velocity*, in 2011. Fortin is also the author of four chapbooks, from Dancing Girl Press, the Dusie Kollektiv, Poor Claudia, and Greying Ghost Press.

With three other poets, she founded and edits *LEVELER*. Fortin is a Returned Peace Corps Volunteer (Bulgaria 2004-2006). She now works in Public Relations/Communications at the University of Rochester Medical Center.

For more information, visit www.jenniferhfortin.com.

H_NGM_N was founded in the fall of 2001. Originally a mimeographed and side-stapled poetry 'zine, H_NGM_N transitioned to the current online format for the journal in 2004.

H_NGM_N Books was formed in 2010 and releases 3-5 titles per year—most of which are selected through our annual Open Reading period (November – March).

H_NGM_N flourishes at the nexus of old tech and new: dittos and screens, human hearts and digital speed.

H_NGM_N is a way of life, a type of attention.

www.h-ngm-n.com

www.ingramcontent.com/pod-product-compliance
Lightning Source LLC
LaVergne TN
LVHW091204080426
835509LV00006B/817